THIS JOURNAL BELONGS TO:

_____

OF THE BOOK CLUB

_____

BOOK CLUB

A JOURNAL

INTRODUCTION

Welcome to the definitive book clubbing journal.

Whether you're a voracious reader now or want to bring books back into your life, whether you're a book club veteran or want to start your first one—this notebook is right for you.

At the heart of this journal, you'll find guided pages to help you prepare for, keep track of, and remember your meetings with your beloved fellow readers. You'll have a tidy place to list questions about what books you've read and document details about the meetings themselves, and plenty of personal space to write your own thoughts, feelings, and memories. And next time you forget who said that Brilliant Thing about That Awesome Character? Just pull out your journal and reminisce.

These pages also include a helpful guide to starting and running a book club, and, in the back, fun activities to kick off your gatherings and curated book recommendations when it's your turn to suggest your group's next read.

Above all, use this journal in a way that works for you and your reading buddies. Sharing your literary life with others can be one of the best decisions you've ever made.

Read on!

—Abbe Wright and Ilana Masad, Read it Forward

WANT TO START A BOOK CLUB?

Discussing books should be an event everyone looks forward to. Check out these tips to begin your club in no time. (And keep it going!)

A BOOK CLUB DOESN'T HAVE TO BE HUGE. If it's you and two family members, you'll have just as much fun as you would with a group of twelve. The most important thing is to have members you can spend quality time with—if you and the other members can never sync up schedules, it's hardly a book club!

BE REALISTIC ABOUT HOW MUCH TIME YOU HAVE TO READ. Do you want to meet monthly, every two months, every three? As long as you make sure everyone has time to read the book and arrives ready to talk, you'll have a good time.

REMEMBER FOOD AND DRINK! Full tummies and quenched thirst make for a mind free to chat. Whether you want to indulge and order in for meetings or make it a potluck where you share your favorite recipes, make sure you have a plan.

CHANGE UP WHERE YOU MEET AND WHO HOSTS—don't stick one person with all the responsibility for too long. This is a group effort, after all. Or meet somewhere neutral like the park or a bar.

CHOOSE A BOOK LENGTH THAT FEELS AVERAGE TO YOU, and then keep most of your book picks at or under that length (and if you pick a long book, give your group more time to read it).

SUGGEST STARTING EACH MEETING WITH SOME ICE-BREAKERS—that way, members who don't know one another well can get acquainted (check out page 000 for some ideas).

ASK EVERYONE TO BRING IN AT LEAST ONE QUESTION TO POSE TO THE GROUP. If everyone does this for each meeting, you'll never run out of stuff to discuss.

GET CRAFTY! Once in a while, bring in a fun activity to do during the meeting—print a coloring page that matches the book's theme, make bookmarks, or bake cookies. Doing something while you chat can help keep your fidgety members calm.

START A SHARED ONLINE CALENDAR and set up email reminders so no one forgets about the next meeting.

CONSIDER A CELEBRATORY AND TIMELY THEME FOR YOUR PICK. Read a poetry chapbook during April, a novel by a queer author during June, a debut by an African American author in February.

DIVERSIFY YOUR READING! Choose a collection of stories to break up a string of novels. Introduce a new perspective with a writer from a cultural background that's different from you. Or switch up serious reading with a light romance.

FINALLY, HAVE FUN and keep it casual!

STAY IN TOUCH

NAME	EMAIL	PHONE

FAVORITE BOOK	LEAST FAVORITE BOOK	ADDRESS

READING
+
CONVERSATION

LOG

Use the following pages like you would a reading log—to reflect and remember your thoughts while reading, so you'll feel prepared for your next meet-up. Then use the Meeting Notes page to track your group's conversation and your club's selection for the next meeting.

BOOK SELECTION

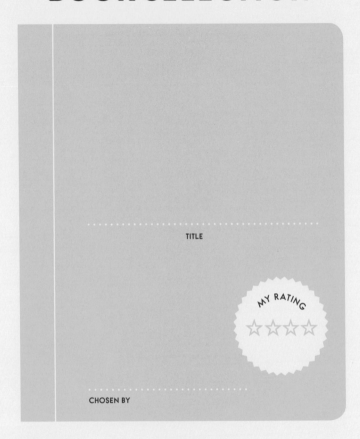

TITLE

MY RATING
☆☆☆☆

CHOSEN BY

GENRE

Biography / Fantasy / History / How-To / Literary Fiction / Memoir
Mystery / Poetry / Romance / Science / Science Fiction / Self-Help
Speculative / Thriller / Young-Adult Fiction / Other

FORMAT

Hardcover / Paperback / Ebook / Audiobook

The most surprising moment:	Quotes to remember:
PAGE	66 99
My favorite character:	My least favorite character:
I like the ending: Y/N because:	This read reminds me of:
Y/N	
I wish I could ask the author:	
	?
Questions for the group:	

PERSONAL READING REFLECTIONS

_____
_____
_____
_____
_____
_____
_____
_____
_____
_____
_____
_____
_____
_____
_____
_____
_____
_____
_____
_____
_____
_____
_____
_____
_____

MEETING NOTES ___ / ___ / ___

BOOK DISCUSSED

_____ by _____

where we met

who attended

what we ate

WHO SAID WHAT

,,
_____
_____
_____
_____
_____
_____
_____
_____
_____
_____
_____
_____
,,

other notes

_____

_____

_____

_____

_____

_____

_____

_____

_____

_____

_____

_____

_____

_____

_____

_____

_____

FOR THE NEXT MEETING

The agreed-upon book

_____

Meeting time and place

_____

BOOK SELECTION

TITLE

MY RATING
☆☆☆☆

CHOSEN BY

GENRE

Biography / Fantasy / History / How-To / Literary Fiction / Memoir
Mystery / Poetry / Romance / Science / Science Fiction / Self-Help
Speculative / Thriller / Young-Adult Fiction / Other

FORMAT

Hardcover / Paperback / Ebook / Audiobook

The most surprising moment:	Quotes to remember:
PAGE	" "

My favorite character:	My least favorite character:

I like the ending: Y/N because:	This read reminds me of:
Y/N	

I wish I could ask the author:
?

Questions for the group:

MEETING NOTES

___/___/___

BOOK DISCUSSED

_____ by _____

where we met _____

who attended _____

_____

what we ate _____

WHO SAID WHAT

,,
_____
_____
_____
_____
_____
_____
_____
_____
_____
_____
_____
_____
,,

other notes

_____

_____

_____

_____

_____

_____

_____

_____

_____

_____

_____

_____

_____

_____

_____

_____

_____

_____

FOR THE NEXT MEETING

The agreed-upon book

_____

Meeting time and place

_____

BOOK SELECTION

TITLE

MY RATING
☆☆☆☆

CHOSEN BY

GENRE

Biography / Fantasy / History / How-To / Literary Fiction / Memoir
Mystery / Poetry / Romance / Science / Science Fiction / Self-Help
Speculative / Thriller / Young-Adult Fiction / Other

FORMAT

Hardcover / Paperback / Ebook / Audiobook

The most surprising moment:	Quotes to remember:
PAGE	" "

My favorite character:	My least favorite character:

I like the ending: Y/N because:	This read reminds me of:
Y/N	

I wish I could ask the author:

?

Questions for the group:

MEETING NOTES ___ / ___ / ___
date

BOOK DISCUSSED

_____ by _____

where we met _____

who attended _____

_____

what we ate _____

WHO SAID WHAT

,,
_____
_____
_____
_____
_____
_____
_____
_____
_____
_____
_____
_____
_____
,,

other notes

_____
_____
_____
_____
_____
_____
_____
_____
_____
_____
_____
_____
_____
_____
_____
_____
_____
_____
_____
_____

FOR THE NEXT MEETING

The agreed-upon book

_____

Meeting time and place

_____

BOOK SELECTION

TITLE

MY RATING

☆☆☆☆

CHOSEN BY

GENRE

Biography / Fantasy / History / How-To / Literary Fiction / Memoir
Mystery / Poetry / Romance / Science / Science Fiction / Self-Help
Speculative / Thriller / Young-Adult Fiction / Other

FORMAT

Hardcover / Paperback / Ebook / Audiobook

The most surprising moment:	Quotes to remember:
PAGE	66 99

My favorite character:	My least favorite character:

I like the ending: Y/N because:	This read reminds me of:
Y/N	

I wish I could ask the author:
?

Questions for the group:

MEETING NOTES ___ / ___ / ___

BOOK DISCUSSED

_____ by _____

where we met _____

who attended _____

_____

what we ate _____

WHO SAID WHAT

," _____

_____

_____

_____

_____

_____

_____

_____

_____

_____

_____

_____ ""

_____

other notes

_____

_____

_____

_____

_____

_____

_____

_____

_____

_____

_____

_____

_____

_____

_____

_____

_____

FOR THE NEXT MEETING

The agreed-upon book

_____

Meeting time and place

_____

BOOK SELECTION

TITLE

MY RATING
☆☆☆☆

CHOSEN BY

GENRE

Biography / Fantasy / History / How-To / Literary Fiction / Memoir
Mystery / Poetry / Romance / Science / Science Fiction / Self-Help
Speculative / Thriller / Young-Adult Fiction / Other

FORMAT

Hardcover / Paperback / Ebook / Audiobook

The most surprising moment:	Quotes to remember:
PAGE	

My favorite character:	My least favorite character:

I like the ending: Y/N because:	This read reminds me of:

I wish I could ask the author:

Questions for the group:

MEETING NOTES ___ / ___ / ___
date

BOOK DISCUSSED

_____ by _____

where we met _____

who attended _____

_____

what we ate _____

WHO SAID WHAT

" _____

_____

_____

_____

_____

_____

_____

_____

_____

_____

_____

_____ "

other notes

_____

_____

_____

_____

_____

_____

_____

_____

_____

_____

_____

_____

_____

_____

_____

_____

_____

_____

FOR THE NEXT MEETING

The agreed-upon book

_____

Meeting time and place

_____

BOOK SELECTION

· ·
TITLE

MY RATING

☆☆☆☆

· ·
CHOSEN BY

GENRE

Biography / Fantasy / History / How-To / Literary Fiction / Memoir
Mystery / Poetry / Romance / Science / Science Fiction / Self-Help
Speculative / Thriller / Young-Adult Fiction / Other

FORMAT

Hardcover / Paperback / Ebook / Audiobook

The most surprising moment:	Quotes to remember:
PAGE	" "

My favorite character:	My least favorite character:

I like the ending: Y/N because:	This read reminds me of:
Y/N	

I wish I could ask the author:
?

Questions for the group:

MEETING NOTES ___ / ___ / ___

BOOK DISCUSSED

_____ by _____

where we met _____

who attended _____

_____

what we ate _____

WHO SAID WHAT

,,

_____

_____

_____

_____

_____

_____

_____

_____

_____

_____

_____

,,

other notes

_____

_____

_____

_____

_____

_____

_____

_____

_____

_____

_____

_____

_____

_____

_____

_____

_____

_____

_____

FOR THE NEXT MEETING

The agreed-upon book

_____

Meeting time and place

_____

BOOK SELECTION

. . . .

TITLE

MY RATING

☆☆☆☆

. . . .

CHOSEN BY

GENRE

Biography / Fantasy / History / How-To / Literary Fiction / Memoir
Mystery / Poetry / Romance / Science / Science Fiction / Self-Help
Speculative / Thriller / Young-Adult Fiction / Other

FORMAT

Hardcover / Paperback / Ebook / Audiobook

The most surprising moment:	Quotes to remember:
PAGE	66 99

My favorite character:	My least favorite character:

I like the ending: Y/N because:	This read reminds me of:
Y/N	

I wish I could ask the author:
?

Questions for the group:

MEETING NOTES ___ / ___ / ___

BOOK DISCUSSED

_____ by _____

where we met _____

who attended _____

_____

what we ate _____

WHO SAID WHAT

“
_____
_____
_____
_____
_____
_____
_____
_____
_____
_____
_____
_____
”

other notes

_____

_____

_____

_____

_____

_____

_____

_____

_____

_____

_____

_____

_____

_____

_____

_____

_____

FOR THE NEXT MEETING

The agreed-upon book

_____

Meeting time and place

_____

BOOK SELECTION

. . . .

TITLE

MY RATING

☆☆☆☆

. . . .

CHOSEN BY

GENRE

Biography / Fantasy / History / How-To / Literary Fiction / Memoir
Mystery / Poetry / Romance / Science / Science Fiction / Self-Help
Speculative / Thriller / Young-Adult Fiction / Other

FORMAT

Hardcover / Paperback / Ebook / Audiobook

The most surprising moment:	Quotes to remember:
PAGE	" "

My favorite character:	My least favorite character:

I like the ending: Y/N because:	This read reminds me of:
Y/N	

I wish I could ask the author:
?

Questions for the group:

MEETING NOTES __ / __ / __
_{date}

BOOK DISCUSSED

_____ by _____

where we met _____

who attended _____

_____

what we ate _____

WHO SAID WHAT

"
_____
_____
_____
_____
_____
_____
_____
_____
_____
_____
_____
_____ "

other notes

_____

_____

_____

_____

_____

_____

_____

_____

_____

_____

_____

_____

_____

_____

_____

_____

_____

FOR THE NEXT MEETING

The agreed-upon book

_____

Meeting time and place

_____

BOOK SELECTION

TITLE

MY RATING

☆☆☆☆

CHOSEN BY

GENRE

Biography / Fantasy / History / How-To / Literary Fiction / Memoir
Mystery / Poetry / Romance / Science / Science Fiction / Self-Help
Speculative / Thriller / Young-Adult Fiction / Other

FORMAT

Hardcover / Paperback / Ebook / Audiobook

The most surprising moment:	Quotes to remember:
PAGE	" "

My favorite character:	My least favorite character:

I like the ending: Y/N because:	This read reminds me of:
Y/N	

I wish I could ask the author:
?

Questions for the group:

MEETING NOTES ___ / ___ / ___

BOOK DISCUSSED

_____ by _____

where we met _____

who attended _____

_____

what we ate _____

WHO SAID WHAT

,, _____

_____

_____

_____

_____

_____

_____

_____

_____

_____

_____ ,,

other notes

_____

_____

_____

_____

_____

_____

_____

_____

_____

_____

_____

_____

_____

_____

_____

_____

_____

_____

FOR THE NEXT MEETING

The agreed-upon book

_____

Meeting time and place

_____

BOOK SELECTION

TITLE

MY RATING

☆☆☆☆

CHOSEN BY

GENRE

Biography / Fantasy / History / How-To / Literary Fiction / Memoir
Mystery / Poetry / Romance / Science / Science Fiction / Self-Help
Speculative / Thriller / Young-Adult Fiction / Other

FORMAT

Hardcover / Paperback / Ebook / Audiobook

The most surprising moment:	Quotes to remember:
PAGE	66 99

My favorite character:	My least favorite character:

I like the ending: Y/N because:	This read reminds me of:
Y/N	

I wish I could ask the author:
?

Questions for the group:

MEETING NOTES ___ / ___ / ___
date

BOOK DISCUSSED

_____ by _____

where we met _____

who attended _____

_____

what we ate _____

WHO SAID WHAT

" _____

_____

_____

_____

_____

_____

_____

_____

_____

_____

_____

_____ "

other notes

_____

_____

_____

_____

_____

_____

_____

_____

_____

_____

_____

_____

_____

_____

_____

_____

_____

_____

FOR THE NEXT MEETING

The agreed-upon book

_____

Meeting time and place

_____

BOOK SELECTION

TITLE

MY RATING

☆☆☆☆

CHOSEN BY

GENRE

Biography / Fantasy / History / How-To / Literary Fiction / Memoir
Mystery / Poetry / Romance / Science / Science Fiction / Self-Help
Speculative / Thriller / Young-Adult Fiction / Other

FORMAT

Hardcover / Paperback / Ebook / Audiobook

The most surprising moment:	Quotes to remember:
PAGE	" "

My favorite character:	My least favorite character:

I like the ending: Y/N because:	This read reminds me of:
Y/N	

I wish I could ask the author:

?

Questions for the group:

MEETING NOTES ___ / ___ / ___
date

BOOK DISCUSSED

_____ by _____

where we met _____

who attended _____

_____

what we ate _____

WHO SAID WHAT

"
_____

_____

_____

_____

_____

_____

_____

_____

_____

_____

_____

_____

_____

_____
"

other notes

_____

_____

_____

_____

_____

_____

_____

_____

_____

_____

_____

_____

_____

_____

_____

_____

_____

FOR THE NEXT MEETING

The agreed-upon book

_____

Meeting time and place

_____

BOOK SELECTION

TITLE

MY RATING
☆☆☆☆

CHOSEN BY

GENRE

Biography / Fantasy / History / How-To / Literary Fiction / Memoir
Mystery / Poetry / Romance / Science / Science Fiction / Self-Help
Speculative / Thriller / Young-Adult Fiction / Other

FORMAT

Hardcover / Paperback / Ebook / Audiobook

The most surprising moment:	Quotes to remember:
PAGE	" "
My favorite character:	My least favorite character:
I like the ending: Y/N because:	This read reminds me of:
Y/N	

I wish I could ask the author:
?

Questions for the group:

MEETING NOTES ___ / ___ / ___
date

BOOK DISCUSSED

_____ by _____

where we met _____

who attended _____

_____

what we ate _____

WHO SAID WHAT

,,
_____

_____

_____

_____

_____

_____

_____

_____

_____

_____

_____

_____
,,

other notes

_____

_____

_____

_____

_____

_____

_____

_____

_____

_____

_____

_____

_____

_____

_____

_____

_____

_____

_____

FOR THE NEXT MEETING

The agreed-upon book

_____

Meeting time and place

_____

BOOK SELECTION

· ·

TITLE

MY RATING

☆☆☆☆

· ·

CHOSEN BY

GENRE

Biography / Fantasy / History / How-To / Literary Fiction / Memoir
Mystery / Poetry / Romance / Science / Science Fiction / Self-Help
Speculative / Thriller / Young-Adult Fiction / Other

FORMAT

Hardcover / Paperback / Ebook / Audiobook

The most surprising moment:	Quotes to remember:
PAGE	

My favorite character:	My least favorite character:

I like the ending: Y/N because:	This read reminds me of:

I wish I could ask the author:

Questions for the group:

MEETING NOTES ___ / ___ / ___
date

BOOK DISCUSSED

_____ by _____

where we met _____

who attended _____

_____

what we ate _____

WHO SAID WHAT

" _____

_____

_____

_____

_____

_____

_____

_____

_____

_____

_____

_____ "

other notes

_____

_____

_____

_____

_____

_____

_____

_____

_____

_____

_____

_____

_____

_____

_____

_____

_____

_____

FOR THE NEXT MEETING

The agreed-upon book

_____

Meeting time and place

_____

BOOK SELECTION

TITLE

MY RATING

☆☆☆☆

CHOSEN BY

GENRE

Biography / Fantasy / History / How-To / Literary Fiction / Memoir
Mystery / Poetry / Romance / Science / Science Fiction / Self-Help
Speculative / Thriller / Young-Adult Fiction / Other

FORMAT

Hardcover / Paperback / Ebook / Audiobook

The most surprising moment:	Quotes to remember:
PAGE	66 99

My favorite character:	My least favorite character:

I like the ending: Y/N because:	This read reminds me of:
Y/N	

I wish I could ask the author:
?

Questions for the group:

MEETING NOTES ___ / ___ / ___
date

BOOK DISCUSSED

_____ by _____

where we met _____

who attended _____

_____

what we ate _____

WHO SAID WHAT

" _____

_____

_____

_____

_____

_____

_____

_____

_____

_____

_____ "

_____

other notes

_____

_____

_____

_____

_____

_____

_____

_____

_____

_____

_____

_____

_____

_____

_____

_____

_____

_____

_____

FOR THE NEXT MEETING

The agreed-upon book

_____

Meeting time and place

_____

BOOK SELECTION

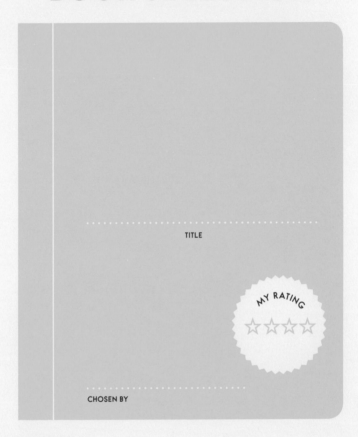

TITLE

MY RATING

☆ ☆ ☆ ☆

CHOSEN BY

GENRE

Biography / Fantasy / History / How-To / Literary Fiction / Memoir
Mystery / Poetry / Romance / Science / Science Fiction / Self-Help
Speculative / Thriller / Young-Adult Fiction / Other

FORMAT

Hardcover / Paperback / Ebook / Audiobook

The most surprising moment:	Quotes to remember:
PAGE	" "

My favorite character:	My least favorite character:

I like the ending: Y/N because:	This read reminds me of:
Y/N	

I wish I could ask the author:

Questions for the group:

MEETING NOTES ___ / ___ / ___
date

BOOK DISCUSSED

_____ by _____

where we met

who attended

what we ate

WHO SAID WHAT

"
_____
_____
_____
_____
_____
_____
_____
_____
_____
_____
_____
_____ "

other notes

_____

_____

_____

_____

_____

_____

_____

_____

_____

_____

_____

_____

_____

_____

_____

_____

_____

_____

FOR THE NEXT MEETING

The agreed-upon book

_____

Meeting time and place

_____

BOOK SELECTION

TITLE

MY RATING
☆☆☆☆

CHOSEN BY

GENRE

Biography / Fantasy / History / How-To / Literary Fiction / Memoir
Mystery / Poetry / Romance / Science / Science Fiction / Self-Help
Speculative / Thriller / Young-Adult Fiction / Other

FORMAT

Hardcover / Paperback / Ebook / Audiobook

The most surprising moment:	Quotes to remember:
PAGE	" "

My favorite character:	My least favorite character:

I like the ending: Y/N because:	This read reminds me of:
Y/N	

I wish I could ask the author:

?

Questions for the group:

MEETING NOTES ___ / ___ / ___
date

BOOK DISCUSSED

_____ by _____

where we met _____

who attended _____

_____

what we ate _____

WHO SAID WHAT

"
_____
_____
_____
_____
_____
_____
_____
_____
_____
_____
_____
_____
"

other notes

_____

_____

_____

_____

_____

_____

_____

_____

_____

_____

_____

_____

_____

_____

_____

_____

_____

FOR THE NEXT MEETING

The agreed-upon book

_____

Meeting time and place

_____

BOOK SELECTION

TITLE

MY RATING
☆☆☆☆

CHOSEN BY

GENRE

Biography / Fantasy / History / How-To / Literary Fiction / Memoir
Mystery / Poetry / Romance / Science / Science Fiction / Self-Help
Speculative / Thriller / Young-Adult Fiction / Other

FORMAT

Hardcover / Paperback / Ebook / Audiobook

The most surprising moment:	Quotes to remember:
PAGE	
My favorite character:	My least favorite character:
I like the ending: Y/N because:	This read reminds me of:

I wish I could ask the author:

Questions for the group:

PERSONAL READING REFLECTIONS

PERSONAL READING REFLECTIONS

MEETING NOTES ___ / ___ / ___

BOOK DISCUSSED

_____ by _____

where we met _____

who attended _____

_____

what we ate _____

WHO SAID WHAT

,,

_____

_____

_____

_____

_____

_____

_____

_____

_____

_____

,,

other notes

_____

_____

_____

_____

_____

_____

_____

_____

_____

_____

_____

_____

_____

_____

_____

_____

_____

_____

FOR THE NEXT MEETING

The agreed-upon book

_____

Meeting time and place

_____

BOOK SELECTION

· ·

TITLE

MY RATING

☆☆☆☆

· ·

CHOSEN BY

GENRE

Biography / Fantasy / History / How-To / Literary Fiction / Memoir
Mystery / Poetry / Romance / Science / Science Fiction / Self-Help
Speculative / Thriller / Young-Adult Fiction / Other

FORMAT

Hardcover / Paperback / Ebook / Audiobook

The most surprising moment:	Quotes to remember:
PAGE	66 99
My favorite character:	My least favorite character:
I like the ending: Y/N because:	This read reminds me of:
Y/N	

I wish I could ask the author:
?

Questions for the group:

MEETING NOTES ___ / ___ / ___
date

BOOK DISCUSSED

_____ by _____

where we met _____

who attended _____

_____

what we ate _____

WHO SAID WHAT

,,

_____

_____

_____

_____

_____

_____

_____

_____

_____

_____

_____

,,

other notes

_____

_____

_____

_____

_____

_____

_____

_____

_____

_____

_____

_____

_____

_____

_____

_____

_____

_____

FOR THE NEXT MEETING

The agreed-upon book

_____

Meeting time and place

_____

BOOK SELECTION

TITLE

MY RATING

☆☆☆☆

CHOSEN BY

GENRE

Biography / Fantasy / History / How-To / Literary Fiction / Memoir
Mystery / Poetry / Romance / Science / Science Fiction / Self-Help
Speculative / Thriller / Young-Adult Fiction / Other

FORMAT

Hardcover / Paperback / Ebook / Audiobook

The most surprising moment:	Quotes to remember:
PAGE	66 99

My favorite character:	My least favorite character:

I like the ending: Y/N because:	This read reminds me of:
Y/N	

I wish I could ask the author:
?

Questions for the group:

MEETING NOTES ___ / ___ / ___
_{date}

BOOK DISCUSSED

_____ by _____

where we met _____

who attended _____

_____

what we ate _____

WHO SAID WHAT

,,
_____
_____
_____
_____
_____
_____
_____
_____
_____
_____
_____
_____ ,,
_____

other notes

_____

_____

_____

_____

_____

_____

_____

_____

_____

_____

_____

_____

_____

_____

_____

_____

_____

_____

FOR THE NEXT MEETING

The agreed-upon book

_____

Meeting time and place

_____

BOOK SELECTION

TITLE

MY RATING
☆☆☆☆

CHOSEN BY

GENRE

Biography / Fantasy / History / How-To / Literary Fiction / Memoir
Mystery / Poetry / Romance / Science / Science Fiction / Self-Help
Speculative / Thriller / Young-Adult Fiction / Other

FORMAT

Hardcover / Paperback / Ebook / Audiobook

The most surprising moment:	Quotes to remember:
PAGE	" "
My favorite character:	My least favorite character:
I like the ending: Y/N because:	This read reminds me of:
Y/N	

I wish I could ask the author:
?

Questions for the group:

PERSONAL READING REFLECTIONS

MEETING NOTES ___ / ___ / ___

BOOK DISCUSSED

_____ by _____

where we met _____

who attended _____

_____

what we ate _____

WHO SAID WHAT

" _____

_____

_____

_____

_____

_____

_____

_____

_____

_____

_____

_____ "

other notes

_____

_____

_____

_____

_____

_____

_____

_____

_____

_____

_____

_____

_____

_____

_____

_____

_____

_____

FOR THE NEXT MEETING

The agreed-upon book

_____

Meeting time and place

_____

BOOK SELECTION

TITLE

MY RATING

☆☆☆☆

CHOSEN BY

GENRE

Biography / Fantasy / History / How-To / Literary Fiction / Memoir
Mystery / Poetry / Romance / Science / Science Fiction / Self-Help
Speculative / Thriller / Young-Adult Fiction / Other

FORMAT

Hardcover / Paperback / Ebook / Audiobook

The most surprising moment:	Quotes to remember:
PAGE	

My favorite character:	My least favorite character:

I like the ending: Y/N because:	This read reminds me of:
Y/N	

I wish I could ask the author:

Questions for the group:

MEETING NOTES ___ / ___ / ___

BOOK DISCUSSED

_____ by _____

where we met _____

who attended _____

_____

what we ate _____

WHO SAID WHAT

,,

_____

_____

_____

_____

_____

_____

_____

_____

_____

_____

_____

,,

other notes

_____

_____

_____

_____

_____

_____

_____

_____

_____

_____

_____

_____

_____

_____

_____

_____

_____

_____

FOR THE NEXT MEETING

The agreed-upon book

_____

Meeting time and place

_____

BOOK SELECTION

. . . .
TITLE

MY RATING
☆☆☆☆

. . . .
CHOSEN BY

GENRE

Biography / Fantasy / History / How-To / Literary Fiction / Memoir
Mystery / Poetry / Romance / Science / Science Fiction / Self-Help
Speculative / Thriller / Young-Adult Fiction / Other

FORMAT

Hardcover / Paperback / Ebook / Audiobook

The most surprising moment:	Quotes to remember:
PAGE	66 99

My favorite character:	My least favorite character:

I like the ending: Y/N because:	This read reminds me of:
Y/N	

I wish I could ask the author:
?

Questions for the group:

PERSONAL READING REFLECTIONS

MEETING NOTES ___ / ___ / ___

BOOK DISCUSSED

_____ by _____

where we met _____

who attended _____

_____

what we ate _____

WHO SAID WHAT

,,
_____

_____

_____

_____

_____

_____

_____

_____

_____

_____

_____

_____
,,

other notes

_____

_____

_____

_____

_____

_____

_____

_____

_____

_____

_____

_____

_____

_____

_____

_____

FOR THE NEXT MEETING

The agreed-upon book

_____

Meeting time and place

_____

BOOK SELECTION

TITLE

MY RATING

☆☆☆☆

CHOSEN BY

GENRE

Biography / Fantasy / History / How-To / Literary Fiction / Memoir
Mystery / Poetry / Romance / Science / Science Fiction / Self-Help
Speculative / Thriller / Young-Adult Fiction / Other

FORMAT

Hardcover / Paperback / Ebook / Audiobook

The most surprising moment:	Quotes to remember:
PAGE	66 99
My favorite character:	My least favorite character:
I like the ending: Y/N because:	This read reminds me of:
Y/N	
I wish I could ask the author:	
?	
Questions for the group:	

MEETING NOTES ___ / ___ / ___
date

BOOK DISCUSSED

_____ by _____

where we met

who attended

what we ate

WHO SAID WHAT

66 _____

_____

_____

_____

_____

_____

_____

_____

_____

_____

_____ 99

_____

other notes

_____

_____

_____

_____

_____

_____

_____

_____

_____

_____

_____

_____

_____

_____

_____

_____

_____

_____

FOR THE NEXT MEETING

The agreed-upon book

_____

Meeting time and place

_____

BOOK SELECTION

. . . .

TITLE

MY RATING

☆☆☆☆

. . . .

CHOSEN BY

GENRE

Biography / Fantasy / History / How-To / Literary Fiction / Memoir
Mystery / Poetry / Romance / Science / Science Fiction / Self-Help
Speculative / Thriller / Young-Adult Fiction / Other

FORMAT

Hardcover / Paperback / Ebook / Audiobook

The most surprising moment:	Quotes to remember:

My favorite character:	My least favorite character:

I like the ending: Y/N because:	This read reminds me of:

I wish I could ask the author:

Questions for the group:

MEETING NOTES ___ / ___ / ___
date

BOOK DISCUSSED

_____ by _____

where we met _____

who attended _____

_____

what we ate _____

WHO SAID WHAT

" _____

_____

_____

_____

_____

_____

_____

_____

_____

_____

_____

_____ "

other notes

_____

_____

_____

_____

_____

_____

_____

_____

_____

_____

_____

_____

_____

_____

_____

_____

FOR THE NEXT MEETING

The agreed-upon book

_____

Meeting time and place

_____

BOOK SELECTION

. . . .

TITLE

MY RATING

☆ ☆ ☆ ☆

. . . .

CHOSEN BY

GENRE

Biography / Fantasy / History / How-To / Literary Fiction / Memoir
Mystery / Poetry / Romance / Science / Science Fiction / Self-Help
Speculative / Thriller / Young-Adult Fiction / Other

FORMAT

Hardcover / Paperback / Ebook / Audiobook

The most surprising moment:	Quotes to remember:
PAGE	" "
My favorite character:	My least favorite character:
I like the ending: Y/N because:	This read reminds me of:
Y/N	

I wish I could ask the author:
?

Questions for the group:

MEETING NOTES ___ / ___ / ___

BOOK DISCUSSED

_____ by _____

where we met

who attended

what we ate

WHO SAID WHAT

"" _____

_____

_____

_____

_____

_____

_____

_____

_____

_____

_____ ""

other notes

_____

_____

_____

_____

_____

_____

_____

_____

_____

_____

_____

_____

_____

_____

_____

_____

_____

_____

_____

FOR THE NEXT MEETING

The agreed-upon book

_____

Meeting time and place

_____

BOOK SELECTION

TITLE

MY RATING
☆ ☆ ☆ ☆

CHOSEN BY

GENRE

Biography / Fantasy / History / How-To / Literary Fiction / Memoir
Mystery / Poetry / Romance / Science / Science Fiction / Self-Help
Speculative / Thriller / Young-Adult Fiction / Other

FORMAT

Hardcover / Paperback / Ebook / Audiobook

The most surprising moment:	Quotes to remember:
PAGE	

My favorite character:	My least favorite character:

I like the ending: Y/N because:	This read reminds me of:

I wish I could ask the author:

Questions for the group:

MEETING NOTES ___ / ___ / ___

BOOK DISCUSSED

_____ by _____

where we met _____

who attended _____

_____

what we ate _____

WHO SAID WHAT

66

_____

_____

_____

_____

_____

_____

_____

_____

_____

_____

_____

_____

_____

99

other notes

_____

_____

_____

_____

_____

_____

_____

_____

_____

_____

_____

_____

_____

_____

_____

_____

_____

_____

FOR THE NEXT MEETING

The agreed-upon book

_____

Meeting time and place

_____

BOOK SELECTION

TITLE

MY RATING
☆☆☆☆

CHOSEN BY

GENRE

Biography / Fantasy / History / How-To / Literary Fiction / Memoir
Mystery / Poetry / Romance / Science / Science Fiction / Self-Help
Speculative / Thriller / Young-Adult Fiction / Other

FORMAT

Hardcover / Paperback / Ebook / Audiobook

The most surprising moment:	Quotes to remember:
PAGE	66 99

My favorite character:	My least favorite character:

I like the ending: Y/N because:	This read reminds me of:
Y/N	

I wish I could ask the author:

Questions for the group:

MEETING NOTES ___ / ___ / ___
date

BOOK DISCUSSED

_____ by _____

where we met

who attended

what we ate

WHO SAID WHAT

" _____

_____

_____

_____

_____

_____

_____

_____

_____

_____

_____ "

other notes

_____

_____

_____

_____

_____

_____

_____

_____

_____

_____

_____

_____

_____

_____

_____

_____

_____

_____

_____

FOR THE NEXT MEETING

The agreed-upon book

_____

Meeting time and place

_____

BOOK SELECTION

··
TITLE

MY RATING
☆☆☆☆

··
CHOSEN BY

GENRE

Biography / Fantasy / History / How-To / Literary Fiction / Memoir
Mystery / Poetry / Romance / Science / Science Fiction / Self-Help
Speculative / Thriller / Young-Adult Fiction / Other

FORMAT

Hardcover / Paperback / Ebook / Audiobook

The most surprising moment:	Quotes to remember:
PAGE	66 99

My favorite character:	My least favorite character:

I like the ending: Y/N because:	This read reminds me of:
Y/N	

I wish I could ask the author:

?

Questions for the group:

MEETING NOTES ____ / ____ / ____
date

BOOK DISCUSSED

_____ by _____

where we met

who attended

_____

what we ate

WHO SAID WHAT

66

_____

_____

_____

_____

_____

_____

_____

_____

_____

_____

_____

_____

_____   99

other notes

_____

_____

_____

_____

_____

_____

_____

_____

_____

_____

_____

_____

_____

_____

_____

_____

_____

_____

FOR THE NEXT MEETING

The agreed-upon book

_____

Meeting time and place

_____

BOOK SELECTION

TITLE

MY RATING

☆☆☆☆

CHOSEN BY

GENRE

Biography / Fantasy / History / How-To / Literary Fiction / Memoir
Mystery / Poetry / Romance / Science / Science Fiction / Self-Help
Speculative / Thriller / Young-Adult Fiction / Other

FORMAT

Hardcover / Paperback / Ebook / Audiobook

The most surprising moment:	Quotes to remember:
PAGE	“ ”

My favorite character:	My least favorite character:

I like the ending: Y/N because:	This read reminds me of:
Y/N	

I wish I could ask the author:
?

Questions for the group:

MEETING NOTES ___ / ___ / ___

BOOK DISCUSSED

_____ by _____

where we met

who attended

_____

what we ate

WHO SAID WHAT

,,
_____
_____
_____
_____
_____
_____
_____
_____
_____
_____
_____
_____
,,

other notes

_____

_____

_____

_____

_____

_____

_____

_____

_____

_____

_____

_____

_____

_____

_____

_____

_____

FOR THE NEXT MEETING

The agreed-upon book

_____

Meeting time and place

_____

BOOK SELECTION

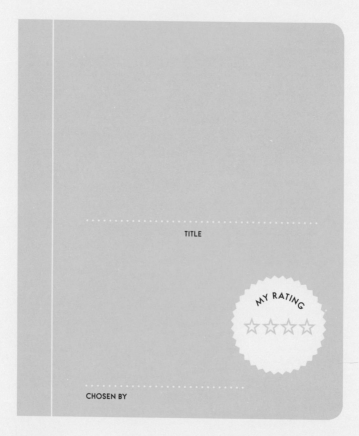

TITLE

MY RATING
☆☆☆☆

CHOSEN BY

GENRE

Biography / Fantasy / History / How-To / Literary Fiction / Memoir
Mystery / Poetry / Romance / Science / Science Fiction / Self-Help
Speculative / Thriller / Young-Adult Fiction / Other

FORMAT

Hardcover / Paperback / Ebook / Audiobook

The most surprising moment:	Quotes to remember:
PAGE	66 99

My favorite character:	My least favorite character:

I like the ending: Y/N because:	This read reminds me of:
Y/N	

I wish I could ask the author:
?

Questions for the group:

MEETING NOTES ___ / ___ / ___
date

BOOK DISCUSSED

_____ by _____

where we met _____

who attended _____

_____

what we ate _____

WHO SAID WHAT

,, _____

_____

_____

_____

_____

_____

_____

_____

_____

_____

_____

_____ ,,

_____

other notes

_____

_____

_____

_____

_____

_____

_____

_____

_____

_____

_____

_____

_____

_____

_____

_____

_____

_____

FOR THE NEXT MEETING

The agreed-upon book

_____

Meeting time and place

_____

ACTIVITIES

In these pages, you'll find ideas for fun things to do during your club meetings. To share with your group more easily, you can download and print extra templates for the following activities at readitforward.com/book-club-journal.

LITERARY ICEBREAKERS

Use these icebreakers in various ways. You can introduce one verbally at the start of every meeting and share your answers. You can jot the responses down for yourself and bring them up as needed. Or you can pass around a single question each week and write down everyone's responses to build a unique reading list tailored for you!

The best book I ever read:

Books I've kept from childhood:

My favorite childhood character:

Circle one:

I prefer to laugh / cry with a book.

I like when an ending surprises me / I can see the ending coming.

I do / do not judge books by their cover.

My favorite book-to-movie adaptation:

My favorite guilty pleasure book:

My favorite reading snack: | My favorite place to read:

The three fictional characters I'd love to start a book club with:

If I had to read one genre for the rest of my life, it would be:

A book that intimidates me (but I'll read it eventually):

I'll never read | I want to reread:

and that's okay.

My go-to book recommender:

Characters I'd most want to be friends with:

Characters I'd least want to encounter on a dark night:

Literary couples that most make me believe in love:

Best-dressed characters I've read about:

The most imaginative settings I've seen described:

The setting in a book I'd most like to visit:

A meal described in a book I'd most like to enjoy:

The best book cover ever designed:

The books that kept me up past my bedtime:

I'm most proud of finishing:	A book I just couldn't finish:

The book I'm most embarrassed about liking:

The most boring book I've read:	The book that made me cry:

The most crush-worthy characters:

The best character name ever written in a book:

MASH (which stands for Mansion, Apartment, Shack, House) is a game that tells your future!

HERE'S HOW TO PLAY:

Fill in the categories below. Then close your eyes and draw a spiral until someone else says STOP. Start from the outside of the spiral and count the number of circles you drew. That's your Magic Number.

FAVORITE PLACES FROM BOOKS:

1. _____
2. _____
3. _____
4. _____

FAVORITE CHARACTERS:

1. _____
2. _____
3. _____
4. _____

FOUR NUMBERS BETWEEN 0 & 10

1. _____
2. _____
3. _____
4. _____

MODES OF CONVEYANCE (I.E. CAR, CARRIAGE, TRAIN . . .):

1. _____
2. _____
3. _____
4. _____

BOOKS YOU CAN READ OVER AND OVER AGAIN:

1. _____
2. _____
3. _____
4. _____

BEGINNING FROM THE TOP, count the answers you've filled out—every time you reach your Magic Number, cross that entry out, and start your counting over, as you keep moving down the list. If there's only one entry left in a category, skip it! Once there's only one entry in each category, fill out the section **YOUR FUTURE HOLDS**, and rejoice (or shudder!) at your fairy tale path!

MAGIC NO.

YOUR FUTURE HOLDS . . .

One day, you'll meet_____ at a bookstore and you
                          (favorite character)
will fall madly in love. You'll ask, "How did you escape the book?" and
they'll say, "Well, darling, wouldn't you like to know!" Together, you'll
take a private plane to Timbuktu, but on the way, you'll crash on a desert
island, and for several years, you'll only have _____
                                              (book you can read over again)
with you for entertainment. But then you'll be rescued! You'll move to

_____ and you'll own a _____ and
   (favorite place)   (conveyance)
you'll adopt _____ of pets, AND YOU'LL LIVE HAPPILY EVER AFTER!
          (number)

BOOKISH BINGO

Circle or cross off the activities and interactions you have during your book club and, at the end of the meeting, see who gets a full row, column, or diagonal to get a BINGO!

BINGO

Laughed til your tummy hurt	Ate savory snacks	Read hardcover	Researched author
Had delicious desserts	Read paperback	Had a glass of wine	Chose a club name
Arrived late	Read eBook	New member joined	Agreed on worst character
Club chose book you already read	Played literary icebreakers	Met on weekend	Argued over best character

BINGO

Learned new fact from book	Brought food	Didn't finish book on time	Book club ran long
Read translated book	Talked about character crushes	Book club read a sequel	Read a short story collection
Forgot book at home	Discussed controversial topic	Listened to the audiobook	Watched movie adaptation
Left item at book club host	Everyone read the same edition	Made bookmarks together	Learned new word from book

ARMCHAIR ADVENTURES

One of the best things about books is that they transport you all over the world, across time and space, and into imaginary and unreal places. Plan your dream vacations with your book club to some of your favorite real and/or imaginary locales.

A CITY ESCAPE

A ROMANTIC GETAWAY

A BEACH VACATION

AN OUTDOOR EXCURSION

A LIFE-CHANGING VOYAGE

A CITY ESCAPE

LOCATION	BOOK

LENGTH OF VISIT

THINGS TO DO

CHARACTERS TO MEET

BOOKS TO READ WHILE YOU'RE THERE

A BEACH VACATION

LOCATION	BOOK

LENGTH OF VISIT

THINGS TO DO

CHARACTERS TO MEET

BOOKS TO READ WHILE YOU'RE THERE

A ROMANTIC GETAWAY

LOCATION	BOOK

LENGTH OF VISIT

THINGS TO DO

CHARACTERS TO MEET

BOOKS TO READ WHILE YOU'RE THERE

AN OUTDOOR EXCURSION

LOCATION	BOOK

LENGTH OF VISIT

THINGS TO DO

CHARACTERS TO MEET

BOOKS TO READ WHILE YOU'RE THERE

A LIFE-CHANGING VOYAGE

LOCATION	BOOK

LENGTH OF VISIT

THINGS TO DO

CHARACTERS TO MEET

BOOKS TO READ WHILE YOU'RE THERE

WHAT TO READ

Need ideas for what to nominate next? We've got you covered with plenty of book recommendations to suit every interest and mood. Take your pick!

THE ULTIMATE BOOK CLUB BOOKS

- O *Where the Crawdads Sing* by Delia Owens
- O *The Great Believers* by Rebecca Makkai
- O *The Mothers* by Brit Bennett
- O *Station Eleven* by Emily St. John Mandel
- O *Everything I Never Told You* by Celeste Ng
- O *The English Patient* by Michael Ondaatje
- O *State of Wonder* by Ann Patchett
- O *Life After Life* by Kate Atkinson
- O *Between the World and Me* by Ta-Nehisi Coates
- O *A Gentleman in Moscow* by Amor Towles
- O *The Underground Railroad* by Colson Whitehead
- O *The House on Mango Street* by Sandra Cisneros
- O *Swamplandia!* by Karen Russell

BOOKS ABOUT SELF-ACCEPTANCE

- O *Untamed* by Glennon Doyle
- O *Professor Chandra Follows His Bliss* by Rajeev Balasubramanyam
- O *Quiet* by Susan Cain
- O *Jane Eyre* by Charlotte Brontë
- O *The Perks of Being a Wallflower* by Stephen Chbosky
- O *What We Lose* by Zinzi Clemmons
- O *Bleak House* by Charles Dickens
- O *The Monsters of Templeton* by Lauren Groff

- ○ *Mr. Fox* by Helen Oyeyemi
- ○ *A Man Called Ove* by Fredrik Backman
- ○ *Gilead* by Marilynne Robinson
- ○ *The Heart Is a Lonely Hunter* by Carson McCullers

BOOKS TO DIVERSIFY YOUR READING

- ○ *The Water Dancer* by Ta-Nehisi Coates
- ○ *Red at the Bone* by Jacqueline Woodson
- ○ *We Cast a Shadow* by Maurice Carlos Ruffin
- ○ *There There* by Tommy Orange
- ○ *Sing, Unburied, Sing* by Jesmyn Ward
- ○ *Crazy Brave* by Joy Harjo
- ○ *Half of a Yellow Sun* by Chimamanda Ngozi Adichie
- ○ *We Were Here* by Matt de la Peña
- ○ *Sister of My Heart* by Chitra Banerjee Divakaruni
- ○ *The Vegetarian* by Han Kang
- ○ *The Sympathizer* by Viet Thanh Nguyen
- ○ *Stamped from the Beginning* by Ibram X. Kendi
- ○ *Redefining Realness* by Janet Mock
- ○ *Without You, There Is No Us* by Suki Kim
- ○ *Fairytales for Lost Children* by Diriye Osman

BOOKS TO CELEBRATE PRIDE

- *On Earth We're Briefly Gorgeous* by Ocean Vuong
- *Olivia* by Dorothy Strachey
- *A Little Life* by Hanya Yanagihara
- *Paul Takes the Form of a Mortal Girl* by Andrea Lawlor
- *Rubyfruit Jungle* by Rita Mae Brown
- *What Belongs to You* by Garth Greenwell
- *Nevada* by Imogen Binnie
- *Here Comes the Sun* by Nicole Dennis-Benn
- *Guapa* by Saleem Haddad
- *It's Not Like It's a Secret* by Misa Sugiura
- *S/He* by Minnie Bruce Pratt
- *Passing* by Nella Larsen
- *The Well of Loneliness* by Radclyffe Hall
- *Giovanni's Room* by James Baldwin

BOOKS TO CHALLENGE YOUR BOOK CLUB

- *The Nickel Boys* by Colson Whitehead
- *The Glass Hotel* by Emily St. John Mandel
- *A Girl Is a Half-formed Thing* by Eimear McBride
- *Hopscotch* by Julio Cortázar
- *The Age of Wire and String* by Ben Marcus
- *Fanon* by John Edgar Wideman
- *Wittgenstein's Mistress* by David Markson
- *Event Factory* by Renee Gladman
- *House of Leaves* by Mark Z. Danielewski
- *The Woman Warrior* by Maxine Hong Kingston
- *Infinite Jest* by David Foster Wallace
- *Grief Is the Thing with Feathers* by Max Porter

BOOKS THAT REVEL IN NATURE

- *Celine* by Peter Heller
- *American Wolf* by Nate Blakeslee
- *Braving It* by James Campbell
- *Welcome to the Goddamn Ice Cube* by Blair Braverman
- *Prodigal Summer* by Barbara Kingsolver
- *Love Medicine* by Louise Erdrich
- *A Room with a View* by E. M. Forster
- *The Yonahlossee Riding Camp for Girls* by Anton DiSclafani
- *Wild* by Cheryl Strayed
- *The People in the Trees* by Hanya Yanagihara
- *The Kite Runner* by Khaled Hosseini
- *The Bone Witch* by Rin Chupeco

LIGHT SUMMER READS

- *All Adults Here* by Emma Straub
- *Such a Fun Age* by Kiley Reid
- *The Gypsy Moth Summer* by Julia Fierro
- *Like Water for Chocolate* by Laura Esquivel
- *The Pillars of the Earth* by Ken Follett
- *32 Candles* by Ernessa T. Carter
- *The Hunt for Red October* by Tom Clancy
- *The Summer Book* by Tove Jansson
- *Born Confused* by Tanuja Desai Hidier
- *Bridget Jones's Diary* by Helen Fielding
- *The Vacationers* by Emma Straub
- *The Martian* by Andy Weir

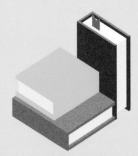

ARMCHAIR TRAVELER BOOKS

- *A Long Petal of the Sea* by Isabel Allende
- *Behold the Dreamers* by Imbolo Mbue
- *The Fortunes* by Peter Ho Davies
- *Today Will Be Different* by Maria Semple
- *Grace* by Natashia Deón
- *Juniors* by Kaui Hart Hemmings
- *Exit West* by Mohsin Hamid
- *Room* by Emma Donoghue
- *Uprooted* by Naomi Novik
- *Under the Tuscan Sun* by Frances Mayes
- *David Copperfield* by Charles Dickens

BOOKS THAT WILL TEACH YOU SOMETHING

- *Dreyer's English* by Benjamin Dreyer
- *In the Garden of Beasts* by Erik Larson
- *How to Be an Antiracist* by Ibram X. Kendi
- *No Logo* by Naomi Klein
- *A Brief History of Time* by Stephen Hawking
- *The New Jim Crow* by Michelle Alexander
- *The Selfish Gene* by Richard Dawkins
- *Orientalism* by Edward W. Said
- *The Souls of Black Folk* by W. E. B. Du Bois
- *The Secret History of Wonder Woman* by Jill Lepore
- *On Immunity* by Eula Biss
- *The Beauty Myth* by Naomi Wolf
- *The Emperor of All Maladies* by Siddhartha Mukherjee

BOOKS TO MAKE YOU LAUGH

- ○ *Dear Girls* by Ali Wong
- ○ *The Pisces* by Melissa Broder
- ○ *My Sister, the Serial Killer* by Oyinkan Braithwaite
- ○ *Eleanor Oliphant Is Completely Fine* by Gail Honeyman
- ○ *We Are Never Meeting in Real Life* by Samantha Irby
- ○ *Is Everyone Hanging Out Without Me?* by Mindy Kaling
- ○ *I Feel Bad About My Neck* by Nora Ephron
- ○ *The Hitchhiker's Guide to the Galaxy* by Douglas Adams
- ○ *Thank You, Jeeves* by P. G. Wodehouse
- ○ *Let's Pretend This Never Happened* by Jenny Lawson
- ○ *John Dies at the End* by David Wong
- ○ *Guards! Guards!* by Terry Pratchett
- ○ *Practical Demonkeeping* by Christopher Moore
- ○ *Holidays on Ice* by David Sedaris
- ○ *Hokum* edited by Paul Beatty

CLASSIC NOVELS

- ○ *One Hundred Years of Solitude* by Gabriel García Márquez
- ○ *Anna Karenina* by Leo Tolstoy
- ○ *Moby Dick* by Herman Melville
- ○ *The Odyssey* by Homer
- ○ *Mrs. Dalloway* by Virginia Woolf
- ○ *Crime and Punishment* by Fyodor Dostoevsky
- ○ *Middlemarch* by George Eliot
- ○ *Things Fall Apart* by Chinua Achebe
- ○ *To Kill a Mockingbird* by Harper Lee
- ○ *The Portrait of a Lady* by Henry James
- ○ *The Tale of Genji* by Murasaki Shikibu

OTHERWORLDLY BOOKS NOT JUST FOR SCI-FI FANS

- *Black Leopard, Red Wolf* by Marlon James
- *Dark Matter* by Blake Crouch
- *The Book of Strange New Things* by Michel Faber
- *A Tale for the Time Being* by Ruth Ozeki
- *Cat's Cradle* by Kurt Vonnegut
- *The Left Hand of Darkness* by Ursula K. Le Guin
- *Ender's Game* by Orson Scott Card
- *Wild Seed* by Octavia E. Butler
- *Embassytown* by China Miéville
- *Oryx and Crake* by Margaret Atwood
- *The Windup Girl* by Paolo Bacigalupi
- *Ancillary Justice* by Ann Leckie
- *The Red Threads of Fortune* by JY Yang
- *Midnight Robber* by Nalo Hopkinson

BOOKS TO READ ALOUD WITH YOUR GROUP

- *Daisy Jones & The Six* by Taylor Jenkins Reid
- *The Female Persuasion* by Meg Wolitzer
- *Little Fires Everywhere* by Celeste Ng
- *BFE* by Julia Cho
- *The Princess Bride* by William Goldman
- *William Shakespeare's Star Wars* by Ian Doescher
- *Alice's Adventures in Wonderland* by Lewis Carroll
- *The Golden Compass* by Philip Pullman
- *The Big Sea* by Langston Hughes
- *The Little Prince* by Antoine de Saint-Exupéry
- *The Joy Luck Club* by Amy Tan
- *Miss Evers' Boys* by David Feldshuh
- *Angels in America* by Tony Kushner

BOOKS ABOUT FEMINISM

- ○ *The Girl with the Louding Voice* by Abi Daré
- ○ *The Giver of Stars* by Jojo Moyes
- ○ *She Said* by Jodi Kantor and Megan Twohey
- ○ *Sister Outsider* by Audre Lorde
- ○ *Gender Trouble* by Judith Butler
- ○ *A Room of One's Own* by Virginia Woolf
- ○ *Woman, Native, Other* by Trinh T. Minh-ha
- ○ *Feminism Is for Everybody* by bell hooks
- ○ *The Second Sex* by Simone de Beauvoir
- ○ *Women and Gender in Islam* by Leila Ahmed
- ○ *Bad Feminist* by Roxane Gay
- ○ *Gender Outlaw* by Kate Bornstein
- ○ *Dragon Ladies* by Sonia Shah

KIDS' BOOKS TO REVISIT

- ○ *Tuck Everlasting* by Natalie Babbitt
- ○ *Harriet the Spy* by Louise Fitzhugh
- ○ *Brown Girl Dreaming* by Jacqueline Woodson
- ○ *A Wrinkle in Time* by Madeleine L'Engle
- ○ *The Phantom Tollbooth* by Norton Juster
- ○ *Charlotte's Web* by E. B. White
- ○ *The Giver* by Lois Lowry
- ○ *Inside Out & Back Again* by Thanhha Lai
- ○ *Are You There God? It's Me, Margaret.* by Judy Blume
- ○ *Matilda* by Roald Dahl
- ○ *George* by Alex Gino

GRIPPING SHORT STORY COLLECTIONS

- ○ *Orange World and Other Stories* by Karen Russell
- ○ *Grand Union* by Zadie Smith
- ○ *Sabrina & Corina* by Kali Fajardo-Anstine
- ○ *Lot* by Bryan Washington
- ○ *You Think It, I'll Say It* by Curtis Sittenfeld
- ○ *Drinking Coffee Elsewhere* by ZZ Packer
- ○ *A Guide to Being Born* by Ramona Ausubel
- ○ *Oblivion* by David Foster Wallace
- ○ *Stories of Your Life and Others* by Ted Chiang
- ○ *A Manual for Cleaning Women* by Lucia Berlin
- ○ *Magic for Beginners* by Kelly Link
- ○ *Self-Help* by Lorrie Moore
- ○ *Night at the Fiestas* by Kirstin Valdez Quade
- ○ *In the Not Quite Dark* by Dana Johnson
- ○ *Pastoralia* by George Saunders

BOOKS THAT'LL TRANSPORT YOU IN TIME

- ○ *Confessions of the Fox* by Jordy Rosenberg
- ○ *Before We Were Yours* by Lisa Wingate
- ○ *Deacon King Kong* by James McBride
- ○ *The Invention of Wings* by Sue Monk Kidd
- ○ *Conjure Women* by Afia Atakora
- ○ *A Woman of No Importance: The Untold Story of the American Spy Who Helped Win World War II* by Sonia Purnell
- ○ *On Such a Full Sea* by Chang-rae Lee
- ○ *Wolf Hall* by Hilary Mantel
- ○ *The Handmaid's Tale* by Margaret Atwood
- ○ *Beloved* by Toni Morrison
- ○ *The Twentieth Wife* by Indu Sundaresan

- ○ *The March* by E. L. Doctorow
- ○ *Time Travel: A History* by James Gleick
- ○ *Dessa Rose* by Sherley Anne Williams
- ○ *The Vagrants* by Yiyun Li
- ○ *The Name of the Rose* by Umberto Eco

BOOKS THAT WILL GIVE YOU A GOOD CRY

- ○ *Educated* by Tara Westover
- ○ *When Breath Becomes Air* by Paul Kalanithi
- ○ *Once More We Saw Stars* by Jayson Greene
- ○ *The Rules Do Not Apply* by Ariel Levy
- ○ *The Year of Magical Thinking* by Joan Didion
- ○ *Marlena* by Julie Buntin
- ○ *The Art of Losing: Poems of Grief and Healing* edited by Kevin Young
- ○ *Shanghai Girls* by Lisa See
- ○ *Fun Home* by Alison Bechdel
- ○ *To the End of the Land* by David Grossman
- ○ *Men We Reaped* by Jesmyn Ward
- ○ *Smoke Gets in Your Eyes: And Other Lessons from the Crematory* by Caitlin Doughty
- ○ *This Will Be My Undoing* by Morgan Jerkins
- ○ *The Notebook* by Nicholas Sparks

ROMANTIC BOOKS

- ○ *The Wedding Date* by Jasmine Guillory
- ○ *Normal People* by Sally Rooney
- ○ *Pride and Prejudice* by Jane Austen
- ○ *The Time Traveler's Wife* by Audrey Niffenegger
- ○ *Tell Me Again How a Crush Should Feel* by Sara Farizan

- ○ *Every Kiss a War* by Leesa Cross-Smith
- ○ *Boy Meets Boy* by David Levithan
- ○ *The Unbearable Lightness of Being* by Milan Kundera
- ○ *Everything I Know About Love I Learned from Romance Novels* by Sarah Wendell
- ○ *When Katie Met Cassidy* by Camille Perri
- ○ *To All the Boys I've Loved Before* by Jenny Han
- ○ *Homegoing* by Yaa Gyasi

GREAT WORKS OF POETRY

- ○ *Brown* by Kevin Young
- ○ *The Crazy Bunch* by Willie Perdomo
- ○ *Devotions* by Mary Oliver
- ○ *I Must Be Living Twice* by Eileen Myles
- ○ *Citizen* by Claudia Rankine
- ○ *Autobiography of Red* by Anne Carson
- ○ *Howl* by Allen Ginsberg
- ○ *Night Sky with Exit Wounds* by Ocean Vuong
- ○ *Leaves of Grass* by Walt Whitman
- ○ *And Still I Rise* by Maya Angelou
- ○ *The Portable Dorothy Parker* by Dorothy Parker
- ○ *The January Children* by Safia Elhillo
- ○ *Saturday Night at the Pahala Theatre* by Lois-Ann Yamanaka

MYSTERIES THAT'LL KEEP YOU UP ALL NIGHT

- ○ *Long Bright River* by Liz Moore
- ○ *Drive Your Plow Over the Bones of the Dead* by Olga Tokarczuk
- ○ *American Spy* by Lauren Wilkinson

- ○ *The Secret History* by Donna Tartt
- ○ *Dead in a Mumbai Minute* by Madhumita Bhattacharyya
- ○ *Shroud for a Nightingale* by P. D. James
- ○ *The Body in the Library* by Agatha Christie
- ○ *Scream in Silence* by Eleanor Taylor Bland
- ○ *Self-Defense* by Jonathan Kellerman
- ○ *Rebecca* by Daphne du Maurier
- ○ *Devil in a Blue Dress* by Walter Mosley
- ○ *Dare Me* by Megan Abbott
- ○ *The Thirteenth Tale* by Diane Setterfield
- ○ *A Crack in the Wall* by Claudia Piñeiro

YOUNG ADULT BOOKS THAT ARE FUN FOR ADULTS

- ○ *Dear Martin* by Nic Stone
- ○ *Frankly in Love* by David Yoon
- ○ *I Am Not Your Perfect Mexican Daughter* by Erika L. Sánchez
- ○ *If You Come Softly* by Jacqueline Woodson
- ○ *Don't Fail Me Now* by Una LaMarche
- ○ *The Hate U Give* by Angie Thomas
- ○ *So Hard to Say* by Alex Sánchez
- ○ *This Lullaby* by Sarah Dessen
- ○ *More Happy Than Not* by Adam Silvera
- ○ *Eleanor & Park* by Rainbow Rowell
- ○ *The Sun Is Also a Star* by Nicola Yoon
- ○ *Hatchet* by Gary Paulsen
- ○ *Shatter Me* by Tahereh Mafi

ON MY LIST

At Read it Forward, we have a healthy obsession with authors, stories, and the readers who love them. Through interviews, giveaways, and extensive book lists, we celebrate a passion for reading in a shout-it-from-the-rooftops kind of way. Read it Forward means we're here to guide you toward a literary future full of books that surprise, inspire, and bring you happiness.

READITFORWARD.COM